# REAL ESTATE
# Exam
# PREP

2nd Edition

## MARYLAND

**Dearborn**™
Real Estate Education

While a great deal of care has been taken to provide accurate and current information, the ideas, suggestions, general principles, and conclusions presented in this text are subject to local, state and federal laws and regulations, court cases, and any revisions of same. The reader is urged to consult legal counsel regarding any points of law. This publication should not be used as a substitute for competent legal advice.

*Publisher:* Evan M. Butterfield
*Senior Development Editor:* Kristen Short
*Development Editor:* Amanda Rahn
*Production Manager:* Bryan Samolinksi
*Creative Director:* Lucy Jenkins
*Cover Design:* Gail Chandler

*Testbank Reviewer:* Kay Hedge
*Question Consultant:* Don White
*Exam Prep Series Content Consultant:* Marie Spodek, DREI

Published by Dearborn™ Real Estate Education,
a division of Dearborn Financial Publishing, Inc.®
155 North Wacker Drive
Chicago, IL 60606-1719
(312) 836-4400
http://www.dearbornRE.com

Printed in the United States of America.

02  03  04  10  9  8  7  6  5  4  3  2  1

# Introduction

**Welcome to *Maryland Exam Prep*!** When you bought this book, you showed that you are serious about passing the exam and getting your real estate license. This is *NOT* an easy test. For people whose test-taking skills are weak, or who haven't adequately prepared, the exam can be a nightmare. For those who have taken the time and effort to study and review, however, the exam can be a much more positive experience.

It's pretty obvious, though, that if you practice and review key material, your test score will improve. This book is your key to exam success.

The process is simple: Just work your way through the practice questions, taking your time and answering each one carefully. Then check your answers by studying the Answer Key, where you'll find both the correct answer to each question as well as an explanation of *why* that answer is correct. It might be a good idea to review your classroom materials and textbook before you start.

Remember: These 200 questions reflect as closely as possible the topic coverage of the state-specific portion of your exam only! For the balance of the test, you'll need to use a "national" exam prep book. And remember, too, that it takes study and hard work on your part to pass the licensing exam: no single study aid will do the trick alone.

Experts who are familiar with the Maryland licensing examination, as well as real estate law and practice, prepared this book. You've taken the first step toward your success as a real estate professional: Good Luck!

*Dearborn Real Estate Education*

1. All of the following would be grounds for revoking a broker's license EXCEPT

   1. being convicted of a felony.
   2. advertising in a newspaper that he or she is a member of the Maryland Association of Real Estate Professionals, when in fact, he or she is not.
   3. depositing escrow money into his or her personal checking account.
   4. agreeing with a seller to accept a listing for more than the minimum commission rate.

2. The real estate commission has the power to revoke a salesperson's license if the salesperson

   1. shows a property listed with a broker with whom the salesperson is not affiliated.
   2. attempts to represent a buyer.
   3. enters into an exclusive-listing contract with the seller.
   4. deposits a buyer's earnest money into his or her own bank account.

3. A broker may have his or her license suspended or revoked for all of the following actions EXCEPT

   1. failing to provide reasonable and adequate supervision over affiliates.
   2. depositing earnest money into the firm's escrow account.
   3. helping another person cheat on the licensing examination.
   4. displaying a "For Sale" sign on a property without the owner's consent.

4. For which of the following acts must the real estate commission suspend a licensee's license?

   1. Not advertising a listing every weekend in the local paper
   2. Causing a payment to be made from the guaranty fund
   3. Suggesting a listing price to a seller
   4. Not taking a listing because the seller wants to price it so high, that in the licensee's opinion, it will never sell

5. Which of the following actions is legal and not a violation of license law?

   1. Encouraging a seller to reject an offer because the prospective buyer is a Methodist
   2. Placing a "For Sale" sign in front of a house after asking the seller's permission and receiving written permission to go ahead
   3. Advertising that individuals who attend a promotional presentation will receive a prize without mentioning that they will also have to take a day trip to a new subdivision site
   4. Accepting a listing where the seller wants $65,000 and the salesperson can have whatever he or she can get over that amount

6. If a broker tells a lender that the sales price on a property is something above its actual sales price, the

   1. broker has done nothing wrong as long as the appraisal substantiates this price.
   2. broker may have his or her license suspended, revoked, and/or be fined up to $5,000.
   3. broker can lose his or her license and be fined and imprisoned.
   4. buyer can receive a higher mortgage amount.

7. A person is convicted in a court of law of providing brokerage services without a license. This person could receive a penalty or penalties from the court of

   1. $2,000.
   2. $2,000 and up to one year in jail.
   3. $2,500.
   4. $5,000 and up to one year in jail.

8. A real estate licensee paid the telephone company to list his name in the directory under the real estate heading as "Mr. Eager, Real Estate Salesperson, Residential Property My Specialty." Mr. Eager is also required to include

   1. his license number.
   2. the expiration date of his license.
   3. his street address.
   4. the name of his employing broker.

9. A real estate conservation area refers to an area where

   1. certain real estate activities are prohibited in order to maintain the stability of an area.
   2. volunteer REALTORS® help establish conservation buffer zones.
   3. the owners may not cut down trees of over six inches in diameter without approval from the conservation committee.
   4. development is limited in an effort to conserve green space and natural settings.

10. When advertising real property, a real estate licensee

    1. may state only the licensee's box number or street address.
    2. may simply give a telephone number to call for more information.
    3. must indicate that the ads were placed in the name of a licensed real estate broker.
    4. must identify the owner of the property.

11. A real estate salesperson decides to sell his own property without using a broker. When advertising the property, the salesperson

    1. must disclose the name, address, and phone number of his employing broker.
    2. must disclose the fact that he is a real estate licensee.
    3. does not need to disclose his license status if acting as a private citizen.
    4. is prohibited from selling his own home in this manner by license law.

12. Listing agreements based on a minimum net return to the seller are

    1. more profitable because no minimum is set on the amount of commission collectible.
    2. legal as long as the seller agrees.
    3. illegal at any time.
    4. permissible with approval of the commission.

13. A seller told a broker that she wanted to clear $50,000 when she sold her house. The broker accepted the listing and sold it for $160,000. He gave $50,000 to the seller and kept the rest. Which of the following is correct?

    1. The broker should have given the seller a better appraisal of the value of her house.
    2. The broker's commission exceeds statutory and NAR regulations.
    3. The broker accepted an illegal net listing.
    4. As the seller's agent, the broker had a duty to sell the house for as much as possible.

14. In Maryland, real estate commissions are

    1. set by law.
    2. set by the real estate commission.
    3. determined by local groups of brokers.
    4. negotiable between the client and broker.

15. Commissions earned by a broker in a real estate transaction

    1. are determined by agreement of the broker and his or her principal.
    2. may be shared with an unlicensed person, provided that this person aided the broker in bringing the buyer and seller together.
    3. may be deducted from the earnest money deposit by the broker at any time before, during, or after settlement.
    4. are based on a schedule of commission rates set by the Maryland Real Estate Commission.

16. A broker received an earnest money deposit from a buyer. Under Maryland law, the broker

    1. must open a special, separate escrow account that will contain funds for this transaction only, separate from funds received in any other transaction.
    2. may wait to deposit the earnest money until the offer is accepted.
    3. must immediately (or by the next business day) commingle the funds by depositing the earnest money in the broker's personal interest-bearing checking or savings account.
    4. must promptly deposit the earnest money into an escrow account insured by the FDIC and registered with the real estate commission.

17. All of the following are legitimate reasons for a broker to disperse escrow money with which the broker has been entrusted EXCEPT

    1. the transaction for which the money is held has been settled and completed.
    2. the broker receives proper written instructions from the owner and beneficial owner as to the lawful disposition of the escrow money.
    3. the advertisement bill for the property for which the escrow is held is due and the broker signs a proper accounting invoice for the accounting department to use the escrow money to pay the bill.
    4. a bill of interpleader has been received by the court, which in turn orders disposition of the escrow money.

18. A broker received a buyer's earnest money check for $5,000 and immediately cashed it. At closing, the broker handed the seller a personal check drawn on his own bank account for $5,300, representing the original earnest money plus six percent interest. The broker

    1. should have deposited the money in a special non-interest-bearing bank account.
    2. properly cashed the check, but should have kept the interest.
    3. should have deposited the money in his personal bank account, and would have been entitled to keep the interest as a service fee.
    4. should have deposited the money in a special bank account, and should have discussed the interest with the parties.

19. A broker manages three residential rental properties for the same owner. One property is in need of emergency repairs, but there is not enough money in the management account to cover the cost. The broker borrows money from the security deposit escrow account of one of the properties to make the repairs. Which of the following is true?

    1. The broker has acted properly by safeguarding the client's interest.
    2. Such action is proper when the same person owns all properties.
    3. The broker is in violation of the statute governing property handling of rental security deposits.
    4. The broker must use personal funds for repairs if there is not enough money in the management account.

20. In Maryland, brokers and salespeople who are not lawyers may

    1. complete a bill of sale after a sales contract has been signed.
    2. fill in blanks on preprinted form contracts customarily used in their community.
    3. suggest additional language to be added to a preprinted sales contract by a buyer or seller.
    4. explain the legal significance of specific preprinted contract clauses to a buyer or seller.

21. All of the following must would be shown in a residential sales listing agreement form EXCEPT

    1. the amount and form of the broker's compensation for selling the property.
    2. a complete legal description of the property being sold.
    3. the termination date of the listing.
    4. the proposed gross sales price of the property.

22. A broker signs a listing agreement with a seller. The agreement contains the following clause: "If the Property has not been sold after three months from the date of this signing, this agreement will automatically continue for additional three-month periods thereafter until the property is sold." Based on these facts, the agreement

    1. is legal under Maryland law because it contains a reference to a specific time limit.
    2. is illegal in Maryland.
    3. is legal because the listing extensions are for a specified three month period.
    4. is legal under Maryland law because the listing period is for less than six months.

23. All of the following would be considered material facts regarding a property listed for sale EXCEPT that the

    1. owner has human immunodeficiency virus (HIV).
    2. property is under construction for rezoning for commercial use.
    3. property has standing water around the house more than 24 hours after a rain has ceased.
    4. property was destroyed by fire but rebuilt on the old foundation.

24. All of the following would normally terminate a listing EXCEPT

    1. the death of one owner who held the property in tenants by the entirety with his or her spouse.
    2. the death of a sole owner.
    3. a disposition of the property through a tax sale.
    4. a foreclosure sale of the property.

25. The Maryland Residential Property Disclosure and Disclaimer Statement is required of the owners in the resale of which of the following, whether by contract of sale, installment contract, or option to purchase?

    1. Unimproved real property
    2. Sheriff's sale, tax, or foreclosure sale
    3. Residential properties of four or fewer single-family units
    4. Properties transferred by a personal representative or executor of an estate

26. Regarding listing agreements in Maryland, which of the following could result in the suspension or revocation of a licensee's license to practice real estate?

    1. A specified commission rate
    2. No specific termination date
    3. No broker protection clause
    4. A specific termination date

27. Under Chapter 7 of the regulations of the Maryland Real Estate Commission, which of the following must be obtained by the licensee agent at the time of taking the listing?

    1. Lead-based paint disclosure form
    2. Property Condition Disclosure and Disclaimer Statement
    3. Stigmatized Property Disclosure form
    4. Equal housing Declaration

28. Upon obtaining a listing, a broker or licensed salesperson is obligated to

    1. set up a listing file and issue it a number in compliance with Maryland real estate license law and rules.
    2. place advertisements in the local newspapers.
    3. cooperate with every real estate office wishing to participate in the marketing of the listed property.
    4. give the person or persons signing the listing a copy of what they have signed.

29. A seller listed his house for sale with a broker on February 1. The listing agreement was to last five months. In April, the seller decided that the house was no longer for sale. Which of the following statements is true?

    1. The seller has canceled the agreement and there are no penalties.
    2. The seller has withdrawn the broker's authority to sell the property but may be required to reimburse the broker certain expenses.
    3. The seller is required by law to leave his house on the market until June 30.
    4. The Maryland Real Estate Commission will decide if the seller's action is justifiable.

30. A salesperson engaged in activities that constitute violations of the Maryland Fair Housing Law, including blockbusting and discrimination on the basis of disability. The salesperson also cashed a $25,000 earnest money check from a prospective buyer and used the proceeds to buy a new car. The salesperson's employing broker was unaware of all of these activities. What is the impact on the salesperson's broker when the salesperson's violations are brought to the attention of the real estate commission?

    1. The employing broker may have his or her license suspended or revoked for failing to provide reasonable and adequate supervision of a licensee.
    2. The salesperson's employing broker will be required to pay any fine imposed against the salesperson out of his or her own personal funds.
    3. The salesperson's actions are legally the responsibility of the employing broker, who will be subject to the same disciplinary action as the salesperson regardless of whether or not he or she knew the violations had occurred.
    4. The salesperson's employing broker will be held liable for the Human Rights Act violations only.

31. A person who believes that he or she has been illegally discriminated against may file a complaint with the

    1. Maryland Board of REALTORS®.
    2. federal attorney general.
    3. Maryland Real Estate Commission.
    4. State of Maryland Commission on Human Relations or HUD.

32. A housing discrimination charge must be filed with the State of Maryland Commission on Human Relations within

    1. 6 months.
    2. 1 year.
    3. 2 years.
    4. 30 days.

33. A broker and an office manager are required to provide reasonable and adequate supervision of all the licensed salespeople and associate brokers within the company that includes all of the following EXCEPT

    1. collection of workmen's compensation from affiliates and payment to the state department of labor.
    2. regular training sessions.
    3. written company and office policies and procedures for the handling of earnest money deposits.
    4. a system for the dissemination of new federal, state, regional, or local laws affecting real property.

34. A Maryland real estate salesperson may lawfully collect compensation from

    1. either a buyer or a seller.
    2. his or her employing broker only.
    3. any party to the transaction or the party's representative.
    4. any licensed real estate broker.

35. When a Maryland real estate associate broker or salesperson wants to transfer his or her affiliation to another broker, all of the following procedures are required EXCEPT that licensee must

    1. surrender his or her pocket card and wall license to the commission.
    2. pay a transfer fee of $5.10.
    3. submit acknowledgment of termination from the current broker on the appropriate form.
    4. submit acknowledgment of affiliation from the new broker on the appropriate form.

36. A licensed salesperson may hold a concurrent license with more than one Maryland broker under which of the following circumstances?

    1. Under no circumstances
    2. With the permission of his or her sales manager and other requirements of the real estate commission
    3. With the written consent of the brokers being represented and other requirements of the real estate commission
    4. With the permission of the real estate commission

37. Several weeks after a closing, an associate broker received a thank-you letter and a nice bonus check from the seller of the house. The associate broker cashed the check because he felt it was earned. In this situation, which of the following is true?

    1. The associate broker may accept the bonus because he is licensed as an associate broker.
    2. Accepting the money is allowed if more than 30 days have elapsed since the closing.
    3. The associate broker may accept the money if his broker permits him to do so.
    4. Accepting the money is a violation of commission regulations.

38. When an employing broker has his or her license suspended for two years, what effect does this have on the associate brokers and salespeople affiliated with the proprietor?

    1. Affiliates' licenses will be revoked, subject to reinstatement after one year.
    2. Affiliates' licenses will be also be suspended for a two-year period.
    3. Suspension has no effect on the affiliates.
    4. Affiliates' licenses must be returned to the real estate commission.

39. A broker intends to open a second branch office in a neighboring town. The broker applies for a branch office license, giving a name that clearly identifies its relationship with his main office. The broker then names a licensed real estate salesperson with three years experience as the branch office manager and sends in this information. Under these facts, will the broker receive approval for the branch office?

    1. Yes, the broker has fully complied with the requirements of the license law.
    2. No, under the license law, brokers cannot have branch offices in more than one municipality.
    3. Yes, by naming the salesperson as the branch's manager, the broker is in compliance with the "reasonable and adequate supervision" requirement of the license law.
    4. No, the broker must also send in $5 for the branch office license.

40. An associate broker is not satisfied with her present real estate company and has decided to become associated with another broker. What is the procedure for transferring to the new broker?

    1. The first broker must transfer the associate broker's license to the new office.
    2. The new broker must notify the commission of the change and send in the proper forms and fees.
    3. The associate broker must take her license to the new broker and notify the commission, within three days, of the transfer to a new broker.
    4. The associate broker's wall license and pocket card, along with the proper fee and form signed by the new broker, must be sent to the commission together with a statement of termination from the old broker or from the transferring licensee.

41. When a licensed broker changes his or her place of business,

    1. the new location must be approved by the appropriate board of REALTORS®.
    2. his or her license would be suspended if the real estate commission was not notified within ten days of the move.
    3. a new license will be issued for a full term.
    4. the new address must be approved by the real estate commission.

42. In any real estate sales transaction that a broker negotiates, the broker is NOT required to

    1. inform the buyer of his or her personal opinion of the condition of the seller's title to the property.
    2. make sure that the written purchase and sales agreement includes all the terms of the parties' agreement.
    3. be careful to have all of the parties initial and date any contract changes and sign any addenda required.
    4. keep copies of all documents involved in the transaction in his or her files for the required period of time required by law, after the transaction was closed.

43. All of the following are necessary for a broker to be entitled to a commission EXCEPT

    1. a written record of all the showings of the property.
    2. a ready, willing, and able buyer.
    3. proof that the broker was property licensed when performing the act of brokerage.
    4. a binding contract between seller and purchaser.

44. According to Maryland real estate regulations, a licensee may have his or her license suspended or revoked and be given a fine of up to $3,000 for failing to maintain records on all of the following EXCEPT a(n)

    1. listing contract to sell or rent real property.
    2. contract of sale.
    3. auto lease agreement when the auto is used only for business purposes.
    4. real property lease agreement.

45. A sales contract requires a termite certificate. The purchaser requests that the salesperson order one. The salesperson does so, knowing she will receive a referral fee from the pest control company. Is this a violation of the license law?

    1. No, if the fee is less than $25
    2. No, if the fee is disclosed, either orally or in writing, to the parties to the contract
    3. Yes, because a salesperson may not receive a brokerage-related fee from anyone other than his or her employing broker
    4. Yes, because special fees may be paid to the salesperson only by the seller

46. An airline pilot, who is not a real estate licensee, told a broker about some friends who were looking for a new home. The broker contacted the friends and eventually sold them a house. When may the broker pay the pilot for this valuable lead?

    1. As soon as a valid sales contract is signed by the parties
    2. Only after the sale closes
    3. After the funds are released from escrow
    4. The broker may not pay the pilot for the lead.

47. A broker is convicted in a court of law on May 1 of real estate trust fund violations. The conviction is final and the appeal period has expired. The real estate commission

    1. must hold a hearing within 30 days to review the court evidence.
    2. may summarily revoke the license of the broker, after giving proper notice of the revocation, and allowing for a hearing after the revocation has become effective.
    3. must suspend the license of the broker, but allow for a hearing.
    4. must hold a hearing before any action may be taken.

48. A buyer has just entered into a contract to buy a condominium unit from a person who originally bought the unit from the developer and has lived there for the past ten years. This new buyer has a right to cancel the contract within

    1. five days of receipt of resale documents.
    2. fifteen days of receipt of resale documents.
    3. five days from the date the new executed the contract.
    4. seven days after receipt of the condominium documents.

49. A buyer has purchased a re-sale condominium and settlement is set for 45 days. When should the buyer receive the condominium resale documents?

    1. Within 10 days of signing the contract of purchase
    2. Within 15 days of signing the contract of purchase
    3. Within 20 days of signing the contract of purchase, unless the condo is being sold by a trustee of a financial institution, or personal representative
    4. No later than 15 days prior to settlement

50. Which of the following best describes the required documents included in a condominium resale package to a buyer?

    1. Condo financial sheet, previous and current year's budget and bylaws
    2. Condo bylaws, plat and survey, and statement of insurance coverage
    3. Condo declaration, bylaws, rules or regulations, statements giving monthly expenses, capital improvements proposed, fees payable by unit owners, and insurance coverage
    4. Statement of financial standing of condominium including the previous and current year's budget, periodic fees of unit owners, and capital improvements

51. How is a broker's commission determined in a real estate listing agreement?

    1. It must be stated in the listing agreement and is negotiated between the broker and seller.
    2. It is determined according to the standard rates set by agreement of local real estate brokers.
    3. If under dispute, it will be determined through arbitration by the Maryland Real Estate Commission.
    4. It must be paid with cash or a cashier's check upon closing.

52. When writing a contract of purchase, Maryland law requires real estate salespeople to use

    1. a contract written by an attorney where the licensee fills in the blanks.
    2. a contract written by the Maryland Association of REALTORS®.
    3. the standard purchase offer and contract.
    4. the purchase offer form.

53. A broker wants to list a property but is getting a lot of competition from other brokers who also would like to list it. The broker offers the seller the following inducement to sign his listing agreement: "If it doesn't sell in 90 days, I'll buy your property." The broker must do all of the following EXCEPT

    1. buy the property at the agreed upon figure at any time during the 90 days.
    2. market the property as if no special agreement existed.
    3. show the seller evidence of the broker's financial ability to buy the property.
    4. show the seller written details of the plan before any contract of guaranty is signed.

54. A broker has obtained an offer to purchase a residence that is listed with his firm. After the buyers sign a purchase and sale agreement and the broker accepts their earnest money deposit, the broker must

    1. deposit the earnest money in the broker's personal checking account for safekeeping until closing.
    2. complete a second earnest money agreement form that states an exaggerated selling price and give the second form to the buyers to present to the lender so that they will be certain to obtain sufficient financing for their purchase.
    3. immediately provide the buyers a copy of the agreement.
    4. file the agreement in the broker's records and, when two or three other offers have been received for the property, present them all to the sellers, who then may choose the best offer.

55. All of the following agreements must be in writing EXCEPT a(n)

    1. exclusive-agency listing.
    2. open listing.
    3. exclusive-right-to-sell listing.
    4. multiple broker nonbinding listing.

56. A residential landlord wants to collect as much security deposit as possible. What is the maximum amount that the landlord may collect under Maryland law?

    1. 1 1/2 months' rent
    2. Two months' rent or $50, whichever is more
    3. Two months' rent
    4. One month's rent or $1,750, whichever is more

57. In Maryland, the age of legal competence is

    1. 18.
    2. 19.
    3. 20.
    4. 21.

58. Which of the following is not a protected class under the Maryland Fair Housing Law?

    1. Race
    2. Handicap
    3. Sexual preference
    4. Familial status

59. All funds received by a broker on behalf of his or her principal must be deposited in an escrow or trust account

    1. within two business days.
    2. within 24 hours on a regular banking day, generally considered to be Monday through Friday.
    3. within five working days of receiving the offer.
    4. promptly, which is generally considered to be 7 business days.

60. A purchaser of a residential property that is leased

    1. would be bound by the conditions and terms of the lease.
    2. could evict the tenants once the deed was duly delivered and accepted.
    3. would be required by Maryland law to give the tenants the right of first refusal.
    4. could evict the tenants after thirty days' notice.

61. Maryland residential landlords may withhold money from a tenant's security deposit to cover all of the following EXCEPT

    1. unpaid rent.
    2. losses due to breach or violation of the lease contract.
    3. cost of repairs or damage to leased properties in excess of ordinary wear and tear.
    4. cost of a stove that was replaced because of its age.

62. Which of the following clauses are prohibited in a residential lease?

    1. Termination of lease
    2. Notice of termination time requirement
    3. Late rent grace period
    4. A cognovit clause, wherein tenants authorize another person to confess judgment on a claim arising from the lease

63. Maryland has all of the following relating to transfer taxes EXCEPT a(n)

    1. 1/2 percent transfer tax.
    2. first-time homebuyer tax reduction act.
    3. agricultural land transfer tax.
    4. Chesapeake conservation surcharge.

64. If a complaint is lodged against a licensee, it will be heard by a hearing board consisting of

    1. at least five commissioners.
    2. the professional members of the commission only.
    3. at least one professional commissioner, one consumer commissioner, and a third commissioner, either professional or consumer.
    4. The entire commission makes up the hearing board panel.

65. The powers of the hearing board

    1. are the same as the real estate commission.
    2. allow the board to administer oaths and hold evidentiary meetings only.
    3. are limited to evidence gathering, but may issue a subpoena in that endeavor.
    4. are to make recommendations to the full commission for disposition of a complaint against a licensee.

66. When the Maryland Real Estate Commission sends a copy of a complaint against the guaranty fund to the appropriate party, the

    1. broker must respond in writing to the commission, giving an explanation as to the allegations and suggested remedial actions, if any, within 20 days.
    2. licensee must respond in writing to the commission, giving an explanation as to the allegations and suggested remedial actions, if any, with 20 days.
    3. broker must respond in writing and supply any evidence supporting an explanation within 15 days.
    4. broker and the licensee both must respond within 15 days and supply any evidence applicable to support their response.

67. If a complaint is dismissed and not referred for investigation,

    1. the executive director may file an exception to dismissal within 20 days.
    2. the complainant may file an exception to dismissal within 15 days.
    3. any member of the commission may file an exception to the dismissal within 30 days.
    4. that decision is final.

68. A complaint is dismissed and then an aggrieved party files an exception. The full commission reviews the complaint. If the complaint is dismissed a second time, the decision

    1. may be appealed to the full commission.
    2. may be appealed to the executive director of the real estate commission.
    3. is considered final, with no other recourse, because it has been considered once, an exception filed, and dismissed again by the full commission.
    4. is considered final as far as the real estate commission is concerned, but may be appealed to the appropriate court.

69. When a complaint is referred for investigation, what must take place before a hearing is held?

    1. The executive director must give 10 days notice to the licensee by regular courier to appear for a hearing.
    2. Proper notice must be given 10 days prior to the hearing and is served personally or by certified mail to the broker or to the broker of the licensee against whom the action is contemplated.
    3. The broker is notified of the hearing at least 20 days before the hearing and must notify the licensee against whom the action is contemplated.
    4. The broker and the licensee must be notified within 15 days prior to the hearing by certified mail.

70. If proper notice has been given to the licensee against whom action is contemplated and that licensee fails to appear for the hearing, which of the following is true?

    1. The commission may hear and determine the case.
    2. The failure to appear is considered "culpability by default" and the commission assesses whatever it deems appropriate in penalty.
    3. The commission must determine the case based on the evidence before them and issue a determination.
    4. The case will be postponed indefinitely.

71. The decision of the hearing board

    1. is sent to the full commission for disposition and penalty phase.
    2. is submitted to the executive director for implementation.
    3. is sent to the chairperson of the commission for final sign-off.
    4. shall be considered the final decision of the commission.

72. If a hearing has been held and a determination made, a licensee or complainant may

    1. appeal to the circuit court of Maryland.
    2. appeal to the full commission.
    3. appeal to the executive director of the real estate commission.
    4. Any of the above

73. The commission orders a summary suspension of a licensee for failure to

    1. identify himself or herself as a licensee when selling his or her own house.
    2. deposit earnest money within 48 hours.
    3. account promptly for any funds held in trust.
    4. respond in the required time to a commission inquiry regarding a complaint.

74. If the hearing board has made a final decision, and a person aggrieved by that decision makes a proper appeal, the decision

    1. may be stayed by the circuit court only upon the licensee posting a bond of any amount up to $50,000.
    2. can only be reversed by the full commission.
    3. may not be appealed as the decision of the hearing board is final.
    4. may only be appealed if bond of up to $50,000 is posted.

75. If the license of a licensee if suspended or revoked, notice of that action is sent to which of the following?

    1. The licensee
    2. The broker of record for the affiliate
    3. The Maryland Association of REALTORS®, the local board of REALTORS®, and any Realtist organization in the area of the licensee's office
    4. All of the above

76. Who keeps the guaranty fund up to its required minimum reserves and administers its use?

    1. Secretary of labor, licensing, and regulation
    2. Executive director of the real estate commission
    3. Real estate commission
    4. Maryland Association of REALTORS®

77. The minimum level at which the guaranty fund must be maintained is

1. $25,000.
2. $250,000.
3. $1 million.
4. $2.5 million.

78. If the guaranty fund falls below the minimum level what must be done and by whom?

1. The executive director must levy the licensees a sufficient amount to bring the fund up to the minimum level.
2. The secretary of labor, licensing, and regulations borrows from the general fund and the borrowed amount must be repaid by the real estate commission with at least ten percent interest.
3. The commission enacts a statute to borrow from the general fund to replenish the guaranty fund to its minimum amount.
4. The commission assesses each real estate licensee an amount sufficient to bring the guaranty fund up to its minimum level.

79. If a licensee causes a claim to be paid out of the guaranty fund, the licensee's license is

1. fined $5,000 for each violation and the licensee must pay the guaranty fund back.
2. revoked.
3. automatically suspended, and the licensee must pay back the guaranty fund with at least ten percent interest.
4. revoked and the licensee must pay a penalty of $2,000 for each violation, and post a bond of up to at least $50,000.

80. Who has the authority to issue a proposed order to settle claim against the guaranty fund?

1. Only the executive director of the real estate commission
2. The real estate commission
3. Only a hearing board who has reviewed the information or evidence that has been submitted
4. The secretary of labor, licensing, and regulations

81. What is the maximum claim amount for which a proposed order may be made?

1. $2,500
2. $3,000
3. $25,000
4. $50,000

82. Who may not make a claim against the guaranty fund?

1. Members of the public since the fund is for REALTORS® only
2. Members of the Maryland Association of REALTORS® since the fund is for the public only
3. Any member of a county or local board, e.g., Montgomery County Association of REALTORS®, since the fund is for the public only
4. A spouse or the unlicensed employee of the licensee who gave rise to the claim or the personal representative of the spouse of the licensee

83. A licensed insurance salesman is also a licensed real estate salesperson. This person used a client's insurance premium to pay for his real estate license instead of the intended insurance. He was found to be in violation of the insurance commission regulation by a court of law and his insurance license was revoked. What action may the real estate commission take regarding his real estate license?

    1. None, the two commissions are totally separate.
    2. The real estate commission must automatically revoke the person's real estate license.
    3. The real estate commission may summarily suspend the person's license.
    4. The real estate commission must hold a hearing to determine if any real estate law or regulations have been violated.

84. What is the ownership limit that associate brokers or salespersons may have in a real estate corporation or partnership?

    1. 49%
    2. 49.5%
    3. 50%
    4. 51%

85. If service of process is made for an out of state licensee on the appropriate party, what is the next step that must be taken and by whom?

    1. The commission must mail a copy of the complaint to the licensee.
    2. The state attorney for the department of labor, license, and regulation shall mail by certified mail a copy to the licensee's broker of record.
    3. The person filing shall submit a copy of the filing to the commission and send a copy by certified mail, return receipt requested, to the principal office of the person against whom the action is directed.
    4. The chairperson of the real estate commission shall send a copy to the full commission, to the broker of record of the licensee giving rise to the claim, and to the claimant.

86. What short-term action may be taken to keep a brokerage firm open upon the death of the broker of record?

    1. Any associate broker may apply for the broker's license within ten days.
    2. Any adult member of the family of the deceased broker may carry on the business of the deceased broker, if they surrender the license certificate and pocket card of the deceased broker and any other information required by the commission.
    3. Any manager of the firm may apply as a substitute broker if they take and pass the broker's exam, regardless of whether or not he or she has taken the educational requirements for a broker's license.
    4. Any adult member of the family wishing to qualify for the broker's license in the short term, must take and pass the broker's exam, regardless of whether or not he or she has taken the educational requirements for a broker's license.

87. What is the length of time for the short-term action that may be taken when the broker of a real estate firm dies?

    1. 30 days
    2. 60 days
    3. 3 months
    4. 6 months

88. What is the purpose of the short-term action that may be taken when the broker of a real estate firm dies?

    1. To allow the substitute broker time to get his or her brokerage license
    2. To allow the substitute broker time to get his or her educational requirements required for the broker's exam
    3. To close and terminate the business
    4. To find a buyer for the brokerage firm

89. What, if any, are the conditions under which a firm may continue to operate after the broker dies?

    1. The firm must be sold within the six month short-term continuation of business period.
    2. The firm must be sold within the three month short-term continuation of business period.
    3. Any member of the deceased broker's immediate family who has been licensed for three years may qualify for the license of the deceased broker subject to other requirements.
    4. Any adult member of the family may qualify for the broker's license to continue the business if he or she passes the broker's exam.

90. What are the additional educational hours required if someone qualifies for the license of a deceased broker and how long does the new broker have to meet the educational requirements?

    1. The new broker must obtain 135 hours of approved curriculum within four years.
    2. The new broker must obtain two 45-hour courses of approved curriculum within four years.
    3. The new broker must obtain 135 hours of approved curriculum within the next year or by the next license renewal, whichever comes later.
    4. The new broker must obtain 90 hours of approved curriculum with two years.

91. The maximum claim that can be paid out of the guaranty fund is

    1. $2,500.
    2. $25,000.
    3. $250,000, and can only be paid for actual losses.
    4. There is no maximum, however, money from the guaranty fund may be paid only for actual losses. Punitive damages, lawyer's fees, or court fees may not be paid.

92. A resident of Pennsylvania has a broker's license in Maryland. The Pennsylvania resident

    1. must maintain an office in Maryland.
    2. must maintain an office in Maryland if Pennsylvania requires nonresident Maryland brokers licensed in Pennsylvania to have an office in Pennsylvania.
    3. must maintain an office in both Maryland and Pennsylvania.
    4. is not required to have a license in any other state as long as he or she has an office in Pennsylvania.

93. A branch office requires all of the following EXCEPT

    1. an application for a branch office certificate on the correct form.
    2. written notice to the commission containing the identity of the individual appointed as manager of the branch office.
    3. an office certificate application fee of $10.
    4. an office certificate application fee of $5.

94. Which of the following is true regarding the office manager?

    1. The manager must report all legal or regulation infractions to the broker.
    2. The manager must forward all complaints sent to the office regarding a licensee who works out of that office to the broker of record immediately.
    3. The manager is responsible for providing reasonable and adequate supervision of the licensees in that office.
    4. The manager does have some supervision responsibilities but most of the responsibility resides with the broker of record.

95. All of the following are requirements for signs EXCEPT that

    1. a sign must clearly be visible to the public for each office.
    2. the sign must be conspicuously displayed on the door or outside of the premises.
    3. the word "real estate," "REALTOR®," or "Realtist," whichever is appropriate, shall appear on the sign.
    4. Only the main office or headquarters must have a sign.

96. The Annotated Code of Maryland provides that unless otherwise negotiated in the contract or provided by local law, the cost of any recordation tax or any state or local transfer tax shall be

    1. assumed by the buyer.
    2. assumed by the seller.
    3. paid according to county custom.
    4. shared equally between the buyer and seller.

97. The buyer's right of selection clause required in each contract contains the right to select all of the following EXCEPT the

    1. title insurance company.
    2. settlement company.
    3. seller's brokerage firm.
    4. mortgage lender or financial institution.

98. Maryland real estate license law is administered by the

    1. Maryland Council on Housing Matters.
    2. Maryland Real Estate Commission.
    3. Maryland Association of REALTORS®.
    4. Department of Housing and Urban Development (HUD).

99. How are members of the real estate commission selected?

    1. They are appointed by the secretary of labor, licensing, and regulations.
    2. They are appointed by the Maryland Association of REALTORS®.
    3. The governor appoints the commissioners, with the advice and consent of the state senate and the consent of the secretary of labor, licensing, and regulation.
    4. The commissioners are elected at-large by other licensees.

100. What is the total number of real estate commissioners?

    1. Four
    2. Five
    3. Nine
    4. Ten

101. A professional member of the commission must have been

    1. a resident of the area he or she represents for at least four years immediately before the appointment.
    2. licensed as a real estate broker, associate broker, or salesperson for at least ten years immediately before appointment.
    3. a licensee for five years prior to appointment.
    4. a licensed real estate broker for at least ten years immediately prior to appointment.

102. All of the following statements are true regarding a vacancy or term of a commissioner EXCEPT that the

    1. length of service for each term that a commissioner serves is four years.
    2. terms of the commission members are staggered.
    3. terms of all commissioners begin on June 1.
    4. secretary of labor, licensing, and regulation may remove members of the commission for incompetence or misconduct.

103. If a vacancy occurs on the real estate commission, regardless of cause, the replacement member appointed shall serve

    1. for the rest of the original term until a qualified successor is appointed.
    2. for a new four-year term minus the months since the last June, if any.
    3. for a new four-year term starting with the month of appointment.
    4. until the next June 1.

104. The chairman of the real estate commission is

    1. solely appointed by the governor.
    2. appointed by the executive director of the real estate commission.
    3. nominated by the commissioners and appointed by the secretary of labor, licensing, and regulation.
    4. elected from among the commission members annually.

105. Which of the following is false concerning the real estate commission?

    1. Two-thirds of the members must be present in order to meet and pass regulations.
    2. The commission shall meet at least once a month.
    3. A member of the public is entitled to be heard on any matter within the jurisdiction of the commission at a meeting of the commission if the public member gives reasonable notice to the commission.
    4. A quorum is a majority of the members serving on the commission.

106. How is the position of executive director of the real estate commission filled?

    1. The executive director is appointed by the real estate commission.
    2. The commission chairman appoints the executive director from a list of three nominations made by the other commissioners.
    3. The governor appoints the executive director with the advice of the secretary of labor, licensing, and regulation.
    4. The secretary of labor, licensing, and regulation appoints the executive director from three nominations submitted by the commission.

107. All of the following are qualifications of the executive director EXCEPT that he or she

    1. should devote full time to the duties of the office.
    2. should possess a broad knowledge of generally accepted practices in the real estate business in Maryland.
    3. should be reasonably well informed of the general laws that govern agency and contracts for the conveyance or leasing of real estate.
    4. must hold a broker's or associate broker's license.

108. Which of the following are surety bonded?

    1. Full real estate commission
    2. Only the chairman of the real estate commission
    3. Both the chairman of the real estate commission and the executive director
    4. Only the executive director

109. All of the following are true regarding the executive director EXCEPT that he or she

    1. serves at the pleasure of the secretary of labor, licensing, and regulation.
    2. is compensated in accordance with the state budget.
    3. may not engage in any act for which a license is required under Title 17 of the Business, Occupations, and Professions in the Annotated Code of Maryland.
    4. receives travel reimbursement according to the per mile allowance of the IRS code.

110. According to the enforcement powers of the commission, it may

    1. not hold hearings.
    2. not administer oaths.
    3. not issue a subpoena for the attendance of a witness to testify or the production of evidence.
    4. seek an injunction against a nonlicensed member of the public illegally providing brokerage service.

111. All of the following are requirements in order for a complaint to be made against a licensee with the commission EXCEPT that the complaint must

    1. give the Title and Section of the Code of Maryland alleged to have been violated.
    2. be in writing.
    3. state specifically the facts on which the complaint is based.
    4. be filed with the commission.

112. Who, of the following, is required to hold a real estate license?

    1. A lawyer who is not engaged regularly in the business of providing real estate brokerage services
    2. A home builder in the rental process or initial sale of a home constructed by the builder
    3. A relative who finds property for the licensee to list and receives a small fee for his or her help
    4. A salesperson who sells a business, such as a deli with no real property holdings

113. All of the following are requirements for a real estate salesperson's license EXCEPT that an applicant

    1. must pay for a credit report.
    2. shall be at least 18 years old.
    3. shall have successfully completed a basic course in real estate approved by the commission.
    4. shall pass an examination given by the commission.

114. An unlicensed individual who engages in activities for which a real estate license is required is subject to which of the following penalties?

    1. Fine not to exceed $2,000
    2. Fine not to exceed $1,000 and one-year imprisonment
    3. Fine of up to $5,000 and/or up to one year in prison
    4. Civil penalty not to exceed $5,000 and a mandatory prison term of one year

115. If a licensee violates a regulation that the real estate commission (REC) is responsible for enforcing, then the REC may penalize the licensee by which of the following?

    1. Fine not to exceed $5,000
    2. Fine not to exceed $1,000 and one-year imprisonment
    3. Suspend or revoke the license and/or levy a fine of up to $5,000
    4. Suspend the license

116. When do real estate salespersons' licenses expire in Maryland?

    1. April 30 of every odd-numbered year
    2. June 30 of every even-numbered year
    3. Two years from the date of issuance
    4. From 16 to 24 months after issuance as stated on the license

117. To renew a license in Maryland, a salesperson must pay

    1. $45 plus $20 to the guaranty fund.
    2. $65.
    3. $95, which includes $20 to the guaranty fund.
    4. $45.

118. A licensee allows his or her license to expire. How long after expiration may the licensee apply for reinstatement?

    1. There is no "grace" period, the licensee must retake the state exam.
    2. Up to four years
    3. No more than 365 days
    4. One year from the last June 23

119. What is necessary in order for a licensee to renew two years after receiving his or her initial license?

    1. 15 hours of continuing education and $45
    2. 10 hours of continuing education and the appropriate fee
    3. 15 hours of continuing education and $65
    4. 6 hours of continuing education, all of which must be legislative update and the appropriate fee

120. How many hours of continuing education must a licensee who is not exclusively commercial and has been licensed for ten years or more have for renewal of his or her license?

    1. 15 hours of continuing education is required for all licensees.
    2. 10 hours of continuing education
    3. 4.5 hours of legislative update and 1/5 hours of fair housing
    4. 10 hours, 6 of which must be of legislative update

121. How long may one's real estate license be left on inactive status?

    1. There is no inactive status; the license is either active, surrendered by the licensee to the REC, or recalled by the REC for inactivity.
    2. A license may be inactive for up to two years.
    3. A license may be inactive indefinitely as long as the licensee pays the appropriate renewal fee and has the appropriate number of clock hours.
    4. A license can be inactive for up to four years as long as the appropriate renewal fee is paid.

122. What is required of a licensee with six years of experience who activates his or her license after having been inactive through two license renewal periods?

    1. Complete 30 clock hours of continuing education, six of which must be legislative update, pay $10 reactivation fee, and affiliate with the broker of his or her choice
    2. Complete 15 clock hours of continuing education and pay $10 transfer fee
    3. Pay $45 reactivation fee and complete 16 hours of legislative update
    4. Pay $45 reactivation fee, $10 transfer fee, and complete 15 clock hours of continuing education

123. A salesperson wants to transfer her license from Broker A to Broker B. The salesperson shows a prospective buyer one of Broker B's listings and goes back to Broker B's office and writes a contract on Broker B's contract form. Was this proper procedure for a transfer of license?

    1. Yes, because the salesperson used Broker B's contract
    2. No, because the salesperson did not get a release from his current Broker A
    3. No, because the salesperson did not have Broker A's release or Broker B's signature for affiliation, nor pay the fee for transfer, nor submit the proper forms and payment to the commission
    4. No, because the salesperson should have transferred before he showed Broker B's listing

124. A woman lives and is licensed in Pennsylvania not too far from Hagerstown, Maryland and wants to sell real estate in both states. For this person to obtain a license in Maryland, she must

    1. first make sure her license in Pennsylvania is current and then get the Maryland license.
    2. claim and pay Maryland income tax on all Maryland sales.
    3. affiliate with a broker licensed in Maryland, complete all the other regular requirements for licensure, and sign an irrevocable consent.
    4. affiliate with a Maryland broker who has an office in both Maryland and Pennsylvania.

125. In Maryland, an unlicensed real estate assistant may perform all of the following activities EXCEPT

    1. compute commission checks.
    2. assemble legal documents required for a closing.
    3. explain simple contract documents to prospective buyers.
    4. prepare and distribute flyers and promotional materials under the supervision of the broker.

126. Regarding licensing and duties of personal real estate assistants in Maryland, they

    1. must be licensed.
    2. may insert factual information into form contracts under the employing broker's supervision and approval.
    3. may independently host open houses and home show booths.
    4. must be unlicensed individuals; licensees must be either salespeople or associate brokers.

127. A man will be retiring in about 15 months. He has completed the basic real estate course for licensure and has passed the state exam. He wants to hold off getting his license until approximately six months before retirement. Can he hold off getting his license that long?

    1. No, he must obtain his license within six months.
    2. Yes, a licensee can delay licensure for up to 18 months after passing the basic real estate course.
    3. No, the licensee must obtain a license within 30 days, but could put his license on inactive status for up to four years.
    4. Yes, a licensee has up to one year to activate his or her license before he or she would have to retake the state exam.

128. Which of the following is a requirement for obtaining a broker's license?

    1. Affiliate with the broker of his or her choice
    2. The licensee must have been licensed for at least two years
    3. Pass the broker's exam
    4. Complete 90 hours of additional REC-approved broker courses

129. A farmer purchased 640 acres of land eight years ago and wants to subdivide half of it into three-acre lots and sell them all to a developer this year. Is the farmer required to get a license?

    1. Yes, because he has not owned the land for ten years or more and he will sell more than six unimproved lots in a calendar year
    2. No, because he own 640 acres for over five years
    3. No, because he is only selling half of the section or 320 acres
    4. Yes, because he has not improved any of the lots

130. The composition of a real estate hearing board is

    1. any three members of the commission.
    2. the professional members of the commission only.
    3. the consumer members of the commission chaired by one professional member.
    4. one professional member, one consumer member, and a third member, either a professional or consumer member.

131. A licensee works for Broker A in the mountains of western Maryland. The licensee also has a summer house in Ocean City, Maryland, where he lives from May until the end of September. The licensee wants to also sell real estate for Broker B while in Ocean City, because Broker A does not have an office there. In this situation, the licensee

    1. may affiliate with both brokers simultaneously if they both agree in writing and sign the proper affiliation papers.
    2. may not affiliate with two different brokers simultaneously under any circumstances.
    3. must declare one broker his primary broker for record keeping, but may otherwise be licensed by two brokers.
    4. may only be licensed in the area of the broker that is his primary residence, usually considered to be where a citizen votes.

132. A licensed broker procures a ready, willing, and able buyer for his or her seller-principal. The seller accepts the buyer's offer in writing, then experiences a change of heart and withdraws the acceptance. In this situation, the broker

    1. is entitled to collect a commission.
    2. is without recourse because the transaction was never completed.
    3. may sue the buyer.
    4. may retain the deposit as commission.

133. A real estate company has entered into agency agreements with both a seller and a buyer. The buyer is interested in making an offer on the seller's property. Can this occur?

    1. No, because the real estate company would then be a dual agent
    2. Yes, as long as written agency agreements have been entered into with both parties
    3. Yes, if the seller has agreed to pay the commission
    4. Yes, if the buyer and seller both give their consent to dual agency and the company broker appoints two intra-company agents

134. A seller's listing agreement has expired, and the seller lists with a different brokerage firm. Jim, the original listing agent, now has a buyer customer interested in the seller's property. Jim

    1. is a dual agent.
    2. cannot disclose to the buyer offers received on the seller's property while it was listed with him.
    3. cannot disclose to the buyer information about the physical condition of the property.
    4. cannot represent the buyer.

135. Presumed buyer agency begins in Maryland when the

    1. agent prequalifies the buyer to ascertain his or her price range.
    2. agent shows the buyer the first house.
    3. license first begins to assist the buyer or lease in finding a property.
    4. buyer signs a buyer agency agreement.

136. A buyer contacts a real estate office and indicates an interest in purchasing a home in the area. The buyer does not want buyer brokerage or representation. A salesperson from the real estate office can do all of the following EXCEPT

    1. provide the buyer with information on properties for sale in the area.
    2. give the buyer information on mortgage interest rates and terms.
    3. reveal the seller's urgent need to move.
    4. provide the buyer with a dual agency consent form.

137. A prospective buyer is interested in seeing a house listed with your real estate company, but does not wish to enter into a buyer agency agreement. A salesperson from your real estate company can show the buyer an in-house listing if the

    1. salesperson obtains the seller's permission.
    2. buyer verbally agrees to buyer agency.
    3. salesperson provides the buyer with an agency disclosure form stating that the real estate company represents the seller.
    4. salesperson provides the buyer with a dual agency consent form.

138. Buyer-brokerage contracts in Maryland

    1. must be in writing to be enforceable.
    2. must be on specific state-originated forms.
    3. are not permitted under the license laws.
    4. are illegal.

139. When taking a listing, the Annotated Code of Maryland requires all of the following EXCEPT that

1. the specific amount or specific percentage of the brokerage fee must be stated.
2. a qualified expert's report of the property's condition be included.
3. the listing should be in writing.
4. the seller receives a copy of the listing agreement after signing it.

140. A Maryland broker may represent both the buyer and seller if

1. the broker belongs to a real estate board or association.
2. the buyer and the seller are related by blood or marriage.
3. both parties give their informed consent for dual agency in writing and are each provided with the assistance of an intra-company agent.
4. both parties are represented by attorneys.

141. Which of the following is NOT a requirement for listing agreements or buyer representation agreements in Maryland?

1. The agreements must be in writing.
2. They must have an expiration date.
3. They must state the amount of the broker's compensation.
4. They must contain the first-time Maryland homebuyer closing cost reduction disclosure.

142. A buyer is interested in seeing a house listed with XYZ Realty but does not wish to enter into an agency relationship. A salesperson from LMN Realty can show the buyer the house if

1. XYZ Realty has the seller's written consent to subagency.
2. XYZ Realty obtains LMN Realty's consent to subagency.
3. the buyer verbally agrees to buyer agency.
4. This cannot occur.

143. In which of the following situations must a seller give a buyer a property disclosure and disclaimer statement?

1. Initial sale of single-family residential real property
2. Transfer of single-family residential real property to be converted by the buyer into use other than residential or be demolished
3. Transfer by a fiduciary in the course of the administration of a decedent's estate, guardianship, or conservators of trust
4. Seller selling his own house in which he is currently living, without the representation of an agent

144. If purchasers receive a property disclosure or disclaimer statement after they enter into a contract, the purchaser may rescind the contract

1. up to five days after receiving the form.
2. up to ten days after receiving the form.
3. up to twenty days after receiving the form.
4. only if there is an inaccuracy in the form.

145. A seller has no knowledge of any plumbing system problems on the property he is selling. In actuality, however, the pipes have seriously corroded and will soon need replacement. In the seller's property condition disclosure statement, when responding to whether the seller has any knowledge of plumbing system problems, the seller should respond

1. "yes."
2. "no."
3. "unknown."
4. The seller would not be required to respond to this question.

146. In Maryland, when a broker is listing a home and the seller is the owner in residence, which of the following statements is true regarding the property condition disclosure statement?

1. The disclosures are optional and the seller may avoid liability by refusing to make any disclosures about the condition of the property.
2. The agent should let the seller fill out the form in whatever manner the seller desires, truthful or not.
3. The agent should fill out the form based on his or her own thorough inspection of the house.
4. The property condition disclosure or disclaimer statement is required by law and the seller must disclose known problems of the house.

147. When a salesperson is working with customer-buyers and they ask to look at a property listed with the salesperson's company, the salesperson

1. must tell the buyers that they must first enter into a buyer representation agreement with another licensee.
2. should give the buyer the agency disclosure form.
3. must inform the buyers, either orally or in writing, that the salesperson represents the seller's interests.
4. may show the buyers the property without making any disclosures about the salesperson's relationship with the seller.

148. Five years ago, there was a highly publicized brutal murder in the front yard of a home now for sale. How does Maryland law view this matter?

1. The murder, no matter how brutal, is not a material fact in the sale or purchase of a home and the licensee is not required to disclose the murder.
2. The licensee would have to respond to a direct question about crime in proximity to the house.
3. The licensee must disclose the murder to any purchaser.
4. The licensee may, at his or her option, disclose the murder to any purchaser.

149. The prospective buyers have been to several open houses today. They walk into your office and say they want to write an offer on a home listed by another brokerage. Which of the following is true regarding presumed buyer brokerage?

1. The buyers would need to fully appoint you as their buyer agent and sign the appropriate documents
2. Presumed buyer brokerage ends when the buyer wants to write a contract.
3. Presumed buyer brokerage ends only when the buyer wants to see a property in your company.
4. The agent should decline buyer agency and work as a co-op agent.

150. A broker took a listing for a small office building. Because the property is in excellent condition and produces a good, steady income, the broker's salesperson has decided to purchase it as an investment. If the broker's salesperson wishes to buy this property the salesperson must

1. resign as the broker's agent and make an offer after the owner has retained another broker.
2. have some third party purchase the property on the salesperson's behalf so that the owner does not learn the true identity of the purchaser.
3. obtain permission from the Maryland Real Estate Commission.
4. inform the owner in writing that the salesperson is a licensee before making an offer.

151. A real estate licensee must give the "Understanding Whom Real Estate Agents Represent" disclosure form to prospective purchasers

1. at the first scheduled meeting.
2. before the buyers are shown any properties.
3. at any open house the licensee holds.
4. before any offers to purchase is prepared by the licensee.

152. A real estate licensee has signed a brokerage agreement with a tenant, who is looking for an apartment to rent. The licensee does not charge a fee to prospective tenants, rather, the licensee receives a commission from landlords. The licensee tells a landlord that the prospective tenant could probably pay a somewhat higher rent than the landlord is asking. Which of the following statements is true?

1. The licensee owes the statutory agency duties to the landlords who pay the commission.
2. The licensee's disclosure to the landlord was appropriate under these circumstances.
3. The licensee's disclosure violated the statutory duties owed to the tenant.
4. Because the licensee is not charging a fee to prospective tenants, the licensee has not violated Maryland's agency statute.

153. A licensed salesperson obtains a listing. Several days later, the salesperson keeps and appointment with an unrepresented prospective buyer at the property and tells her, "I am the listing agent for this property, and so I'm very familiar with it." Under these circumstances, the salesperson

    1. has failed so far to properly disclose his or her agency relationship.
    2. has properly disclosed his or her agency relationship with the seller.
    3. is in violation of Maryland regulations because the listing belongs to the broker.
    4. has created a dual agency, which is a violation of Maryland regulations.

154. A real estate broker representing a seller knows that the property has a cracked foundation and that its former owner committed suicide in the kitchen. The broker must disclose

    1. both facts.
    2. the suicide, but not the foundation.
    3. the cracked foundation, but not the suicide.
    4. neither fact.

155. A broker has entered a listing agreement with a seller. Another broker, who has been working with a buyer, learns of the property through the MLS. The buyer has signed an agency disclosure form but nothing else. Typically the second, cooperating broker would represent the

    1. seller as a subagent.
    2. buyer as an agent.
    3. buyer as a subagent.
    4. buyer as presumed buyer agent.

156. Which of the disclosure forma is needed in every residential sales transaction?

    1. Lead-based paint disclosure for a house built in 1979
    2. Agency disclosure form
    3. High tension electrical power lines disclosure
    4. Airport and heliport locations disclosure

157. A buyer is interested in seeing a house listed with XYZ Realty but does not wish to enter an agency relationship. A salesperson from LMN Realty can show the buyer the house if

    1. XYZ Realty obtains the seller's written consent to subagency, and the buyer is given an agency disclosure notice stating that LMN Realty represents the seller.
    2. XYZ Realty obtains LMN Realty's consent to subagency and the buyer is given an agency disclosure notice stating the XYZ Realty represents the seller.
    3. the buyer verbally agrees to buyer agency.
    4. The LMN salesperson may not show the XYZ Realty's property in this situation.

158. A new home developer offers a $1,000 bonus to any licensee who sells one of his new homes in the month of August. The developer's hostess asks the licensee how she would like the bonus. How should the licensee respond?

    1. "In a separate check made out to me."
    2. "In large bills."
    3. "All in the check to my broker."
    4. "All in the same check that you make out to me."

159. Owners of residential rental properties built before 1950 are required to register their properties with the Maryland Department of the Environment

    1. one time and pay $150 for each unit.
    2. once, but pay an annual fee of $10 per unit.
    3. each year and pay a one time fee of $100 per unit.
    4. every other year and pay a one time fee of $50 per unit.

160. In order for a licensed salesperson or associate broker to sell real property, the licensee must

    1. receive their license from the department of labor.
    2. affiliate with the broker of his or her choice.
    3. provide brokerage service only in the name of their associate real estate broker.
    4. join the Maryland Association of REALTORS®.

161. In Maryland, a broker represents

    1. the one who signs a written representation agreement.
    2. the seller, since the seller is the common source of payment, even for a buyer broker.
    3. the one who agrees to pay them.
    4. All of the above

162. A salesperson has shown a buyer a home listed by another real estate company. The buyer has been shown the agency disclosure form and refused buyer agency. Under these circumstances, the salesperson represents

    1. both buyer and seller.
    2. the buyer.
    3. the seller.
    4. neither buyer nor seller.

163. A buyer walks into a real estate company and says to an agent on duty, "I want to see one of your listings." Which of the following is true regarding presumed buyer brokerage?

    1. Presumed buyer brokerage begins the moment a member of the public asks for help, so the agent represents the buyer.
    2. The agent is a dual agent.
    3. The agent could be an intra-company agent in this case.
    4. The agent represents the seller.

164. All of the following are true regarding confidentiality EXCEPT that information gained

    1. while representing the seller must not be disclosed in a way that is adverse to the interests of the seller.
    2. during presumed buyer agency must not be disclosed in a way that is adverse to the interests of the buyer.
    3. during presumed buyer agency may be disclosed if the buyer later rejects buyer representation.
    4. during representation must be held confidential even after the transaction has settled.

165. In Maryland, an unlicensed personal assistant may NOT do which of the following?

   1. Answer the telephone and forward calls to a licensee
   2. Assemble documents for closing
   3. Prepare promotional materials or ads as he or she sees fit
   4. Compute commission checks

166. If there is a dispute about a commission between two cooperating REALTOR® brokers, the brokers should

   1. apply to the real estate commission for arbitration.
   2. apply to the Maryland State Attorney for relief or arbitration.
   3. apply to the executive director for binding arbitration.
   4. submit the dispute for arbitration to the respective board or association of REALTORS®.

167. In Maryland, what is the statutory usury ceiling on first mortgage loans secured by real estate?

   1. 10 percent
   2. 15 percent
   3. 22 percent
   4. There is none.

168. In Maryland, what is the statutory usury ceiling on second or successive mortgage loans secured by real estate?

   1. There is no usury in Maryland on any loan that is secured by real estate.
   2. 15 percent
   3. 22 percent
   4. 24 percent

169. People who are responsible for distribution of funds from a settlement at which a transfer of title has taken place must deliver a recorded release of mortgage to the sellers within

   1. 10 days.
   2. 15 days.
   3. 20 days.
   4. 30 days.

170. In Maryland, sellers who take back a second mortgage with a balloon clause are required to

   1. record and insure the mortgage.
   2. grant a one-time extension of 60 days.
   3. grant an automatic one-time extension of six months.
   4. not pursue foreclosure until the mortgagor is three months in default.

171. By federal law, all owners/sellers must provide the closing agent with the seller's

   1. forwarding address only.
   2. documentation of capital gains.
   3. forwarding address and Social Security number.
   4. bank account number into which net proceeds of sale may be wired.

172. A broker or salesperson may perform all of the following in preparation for the closing EXCEPT

    1. maintain a time schedule and provide net data.
    2. explain closing procedures to both buyer and seller and anticipate decision-making alternatives.
    3. coordinate inspections and deliver documents and escrow monies to the appropriate attorney.
    4. conduct any title searches that might be required.

173. Maryland law prohibits lenders from refusing loans to any person based solely on which of the following?

    1. Geographic area, neighborhood, sex, marital status
    2. Race, color, religion, age, national origin
    3. Disability, marital status, familial status
    4. All of the above

174. In Maryland, when a married couple who held real property as tenants by the entirety gets a divorce, the couple is most likely to hold the property after the divorce as

    1. separated tenants by the entirety.
    2. tenants in common.
    3. joint tenants with right of survivorship.
    4. life tenants.

175. In Maryland, time-share developers must register with the

    1. executive director of the real estate commission.
    2. chairperson of the real estate commission.
    3. real estate commission.
    4. secretary of labor, licensing, and regulations.

176. A time-share developer is required to make annual reports until the developer owns

    1. less than 50%.
    2. less than 49%.
    3. less than 25%.
    4. less that 15%.

177. Upon or before the signing of a sales contract, a time-share developer must deliver to each purchaser a

    1. public offering statement.
    2. statement of holdings.
    3. registration of buildings.
    4. declaration of the project.

178. How many days, if any, do time-share purchasers have to cancel their contract of purchase from its developer?

    1. None, a signed and accepted contract is fully formed and enforceable.
    2. Five business days
    3. Ten calendar days
    4. Fifteen calendar days

179. The right of cancellation of a contract purchasing a timeshare from a developer

    1. can be waived by purchasers by written authorization.
    2. can be waived but there must be valuable incentive made to the purchaser, and the purchaser must waive the cancellation clause in writing.
    3. cannot be waived.
    4. cannot be waived by purchasers, but in some rare cases the right of cancellation may not be offered by some time-share developers who in turn must state that fact in the public offering statement.

180. All of the following forms of ownership are recognized in Maryland EXCEPT

    1. community property.
    2. tenancy in common.
    3. tenancy by the entirety.
    4. trust.

181. All of the following are characteristics of tenancy by the entirety EXCEPT that it

    1. gives a married couple the appropriate estate granted in the habendum clause.
    2. may not be partitioned.
    3. continues even upon the death of one of the owners.
    4. is meant for married couples only.

182. If an owner of a large apartment complex wants to convert to condominiums, the owner/developer must register with the

    1. real estate commission.
    2. secretary of state.
    3. executive director.
    4. local board of REALTORS®.

183. How old must a citizen of Maryland be before he or she may prepare a legally binding will?

    1. 15 (as long as real property is not involved)
    2. 18
    3. 21
    4. Any age as long as the will is legally witnessed and recorded

184. Maryland recognizes which one of the following?

    1. Curtesy
    2. Dower
    3. Homestead
    4. None of the above

185. Legal descriptions in Maryland are based on which of the following?

    1. Government/rectangular survey system
    2. Lot and block numbers and/or metes and bounds
    3. Metes and bounds
    4. The house number and street address assigned by the governmental agency MNPPC (Maryland National Park and Planning Commission)

186. In Maryland, who has taxing authority on real property owned in the state?

    1. Incorporated cities
    2. Counties
    3. The state government
    4. All of the above

187. Under the statute of limitations in Maryland, a contractor must record a notice of a mechanic's lien within

    1. 60 days.
    2. 90 days.
    3. 180 days.
    4. 270 days.

188. After filing a lien, a mechanic or vendor has to petition the court to enforce the lien within

    1. three months.
    2. six months.
    3. nine months.
    4. one year.

189. A buyer has never owned a home in Maryland. On January 5 of this year he bought a home for $180,000. How much is the state transfer tax and who has to pay it?

    1. $900 will be paid by the seller on January 5.
    2. $450 will be paid by the buyer and $450 will be paid by the seller. The total amount of $900 will be held in escrow by the settlement attorney until July 1.
    3. $450 will be paid by the seller on January 5.
    4. $900 will be paid by the buyer on January 5 and is tax deductible on the federal and state tax return.

190. To gain an easement by prescription in Maryland, the adverse user must use another's land continuously for at least

    1. 100 months.
    2. 10 years.
    3. 15 years.
    4. 20 years.

191. The prescriptive period in the state of Maryland to acquire title to real property by adverse possession is

    1. 7 years.
    2. 10 years.
    3. 15 years.
    4. 20 years

192. To acquire land by adverse possession requires use of land

    1. with the owner's permission.
    2. for a period of 30 years.
    3. privately so as to avoid being seen.
    4. without the owner's permission.

193. Under summary process, if an evicted tenant does not remove his or her belongings, the belongings of the evicted tenant may be

    1. used by the landlord.
    2. sold by the landlord.
    3. placed on the street by the sheriff.
    4. brought to the town dump.

194. How must a landlord handle a residential security deposit?

    1. It can be used only for residential units.
    2. Landlords must deposit the security deposit in a non-interest bearing account.
    3. At the end of the lease, the landlord cannot apply the security deposit to rent owed by the tenant.
    4. Unless there have been damages, the landlord must return the security deposit to the tenant within 45 days of the end of the lease.

195. If a lease runs for longer than seven years, it must be

    1. written, acknowledged, and recorded.
    2. written and recorded.
    3. written.
    4. recorded.

196. If an owner defaults on his or her mortgage loan and the property is ordered sold at a foreclosure sale at some future date, the owner may redeem the property

    1. prior to the sale, under the statutory right of redemption.
    2. prior to the sale, under the equitable right of redemption.
    3. after the sale, under the statutory right of redemption.
    4. after the sale, under the statutory right of reinstatement.

197. If there is no redemption after a property tax lien is sold at a tax sale, how long must a tax sale purchaser wait before starting action to obtain title to the land?

    1. Two years after the unpaid taxes are due
    2. Six months from the date of the tax sale
    3. Three years from the date of the tax sale
    4. Two years from the date of the tax sale

198. The transfer tax levied by the state on the buyer or seller of the property is based on

    1. the selling price.
    2. earnest money.
    3. the amount of the mortgage.
    4. the date of the purchase.

199. All of the following properties are exempt from paying general real estate taxes EXCEPT

    1. cemeteries.
    2. federal government buildings.
    3. housing owned by a disabled veteran.
    4. private schools.

200. What is the state transfer tax on a property that sells for $250,000?

    1. $125
    2. $250
    3. $500
    4. $1,250

201. A husband and wife, who own their home as tenants by the entireties, obtain a divorce. At that time, the tenancy by the entireties

    1. extinguishes and becomes a tenancy in common.
    2. continues until one of them dies.
    3. extinguishes and becomes a tenancy at sufferance.
    4. reverts to common interest ownership.

# Answer Key

1.  4.  Commission rates are always negotiable between the seller and the broker, so accepting a higher rate is perfectly legal. The real estate commission may revoke a license if the licensee has been convicted of a felony, false advertising, or commingling of funds.

2.  4.  Salespersons are not authorized to have brokerage trust accounts. No licensees may place funds of others entrusted to their care into their own personal accounts. A salesperson may show and co-op with other brokers, represent the buyers, and enter into an exclusive-right-to-sell listings on behalf of their brokers.

3.  2.  Depositing earnest money into the firm's escrow account is proper procedure. Failing to provide reasonable and adequate supervision over affiliates, helping someone cheat on the real estate exam, and putting up a "For Sale" sign without the owner's permission are all subject to disciplinary actions.

4.  2.  If the commission orders payment by the guaranty fund of a claim based on an act or omission for which a licensee is responsible, the commission shall immediately suspend the license of the licensee.

5.  2.  If the seller gives permission for a "For Sale" sign on the property, the licensee is wise to place one. A licensee is subject to disciplinary action for suggesting that a seller refuse an offer based on religious grounds, accepting a net listing, or for incorrect advertising.

6.  2.  It is illegal for a licensee to misrepresent the sales price of a property.

7.  4.  The court could penalize unlicensed individuals who provide brokerage services with a fine up to $5,000 and up to one year in jail.

8.  4.  Mr. Eager must indicate the name of his employing broker. He is not required to insert his license number, expiration date of license, or his street address.

9.  1.  A real estate conservation area refers to an area where certain real estate activities are prohibited in order to stabilize the neighborhood, e.g. no "For Sale" signs.

10. 3.  All advertisements must be done in the name of the broker. The ad does not have to include the licensee's box number, street address, or telephone number, or identify the owner of the property.

11. 2.  Although there are no specific references to this in Title 17 or the regulations, the commission requires that when acting as a private citizen, the salesperson must disclose license status in advertising. The licensee does not have to include the name, address, and phone number of his employing broker in the ad.

12. 3.  Net listings are illegal because of the potential conflict of interest for the broker.

13. 3. The broker accepted a "net listing" which is illegal in Maryland. This is a good example of the potential conflict of interest that arises in a net listing as the broker was clearly not acting in the best interests of his client.

14. 4. Commissions are always negotiable between the principal and the agent.

15. 1. Commissions are always negotiable between the principal and the agent and are not determined by custom or law, may not be shared with an unlicensed party, and may not be deducted from the earnest money deposit before settlement.

16. 2. In October of 1986, the Maryland Real Estate Commission agreed to contract language that allows brokers to hold escrow monies until the seller executes and accepts the contract.

17. 3. A broker may not use escrow monies to pay bills. The broker must wait until the transaction is completed or the money released by the principals, until he has received proper written instructions from the owner or beneficial owner, or received court instructions after an interpleader has been filed.

18. 1. Brokers must deposit earnest money deposits in non-interest-bearing accounts unless instructed in writing by both the owner and the beneficial owner to do otherwise.

19. 3. The broker, acting for the owner, violated the law by withdrawing money from the trust accounts for this purpose. The money is held for the tenants and is to be returned to them at the end of their lease term, less costs of repair in excess of normal wear and tear and any unpaid rent.

20. 2. The blanks on preprinted forms may be filled in at the direction of the consumers who make final decisions and sign the contract. Real estate licensees who are not lawyers must be careful to avoid any appearance of the unauthorized practice of law.

21. 2. A legal description is not mandatory, but an adequate description, such as the property address, is required. Listings must have a definite termination date, asking price, and definable brokerage fee.

22. 2. Rollover extensions are not permitted under Maryland law. Listings must contain a definite termination date.

23.  1.  A licensee may not be held liable for not disclosing that an owner of a listed property has or had human immunodeficiency virus (HIV). Material facts that must be disclosed include the fact that the property may be rezoned to commercial, has standing water after rains, and that the property was rebuilt on the old foundation.

24.  1.  The death of one spouse who held property by tenants by the entirety with his or her spouse would mean that the property was now held in severalty by the surviving spouse and would not terminate the listing. Termination would occur with the death of the sole owner, a tax sale, or a foreclosure sale.

25.  3.  The Disclosure and Disclaimer Statement is required in the sale of residential real property improved by four or fewer single-family units. There are over 30 exceptions. See Real Property Article 10-702 and Tax-Property Article 13-207.

26.  2.  Not including a specific termination date could be grounds for license suspension or revocation.

27.  2.  State law requires that the seller make known any material defects to the property. The lead-based paint hazard disclosure must be made prior to contract signing, but does not have to accompany the listing agreement. A listing does not have to contain an equal housing statement or anything about stigmatized property.

28.  4.  A licensee is required to promptly furnish a copy of the listing to the seller.

29.  2.  The listing agreement may be canceled but the seller may be responsible for some expenses.

30.  1.  Brokers are required to provide reasonable and adequate supervision over their affiliates at all times, and may therefore be subject to license suspension or revocation in cases where their salespersons engage in illegal behavior.

31.  4.  Fair Housing complaints are generally directed to HUD or the State of Maryland Commission on Human Relations. REALTOR® organizations do not receive discrimination complaints.

32.  2.  A person has one year to file a complaint with the State of Maryland Commission on Human Relations.

33.  1.  A licensee is treated as a non-employee for tax purposes. Therefore, the broker would not pay or collect workmen's compensation. The broker should provide regular training sessions, written policy and procedures, and a system for regular law updates.

34.  2.  Salespeople may collect compensation only from their employing brokers.

35. 2. The transfer of affiliation is $10. The transferring licensee must surrender his or her pocket card and wall license to the commission and submit a termination from the current broker and acknowledgement of affiliation from the new broker on the proper forms.

36. 3. The licensee must submit written consent from all brokers involved, as well as a $45 license fee.

37. 4. Cashing this check was a violation of the commission regulations. A salesperson or association broker may collect a fee only from his or her employing broker.

38. 4. The affiliates' licenses must be returned to the real estate commission These licenses are on inactive status until "hired" by a new broker.

39. 4. The manager of a branch office may be an associate broker or a salesperson with at least three years experience. The broker must also send to the real estate commission on the appropriate form, an application for a branch office certificate, $5, and the identity of the branch office manager.

40. 4. The old licenses must be returned to the commission along with proper fee and form signed by the new broker together with a statement of termination from the old broker or from the transferring licensee.

41. 2. The broker must promptly notify the real estate commission within ten days of any change of business location. The board of REALTORS® is a professional trade organization and would not approve location changes. The license is renewed for the remaining length of time on the previous office license.

42. 1. The broker may not offer a title opinion, which is an authorized practice of law. The broker should ensure that the purchase and sales agreement includes all agreed upon terms and that both parties have copies. Finally, the broker must keep copies on file as required by law.

43. 1. Any action by a broker for commission requires that the broker was licensed when offering to perform and when performing the act of brokerage, that the broker had a proper agency agreement setting forth the broker'' compensation and that the broker produced a ready, willing, and able buyer to buy on terms which the seller accepted.

44. 3. A real estate licensee is not required to keep copies of personal transactions. Maintaining transaction records is required under Business Occupations and Professions Article, Title 17 paragraph 322 of the Annotated Code of Maryland.

45. 3. A salesperson may not accept a fee for brokerage-related services from anyone other than his or her employing broker.

46. 4. A broker may pay a referral fee only to someone who holds a real estate license. The broker can say only "thank you."

47. 2. The real estate commission may summarily revoke the license of the broker, upon proper notice and allowing for a hearing after the effective date of the revocation.

48. 4. The buyer must receive the condo documents at least 15 days prior to settlement and may void the contract for 7 days after receipt.

49. 4. The buyer must receive the condo resale documents at least 15 days prior to settlement and may void the contract for 7 days after receipt.

50. 3. The condominium resale package must include the condominium declaration, bylaws, rules or regulations, statement giving monthly expenses, proposed capital improvements, fees payable by unit owners, financial statements of the condominium, and insurance coverage.

51. 1. The commission paid to a broker is always negotiated between the agent and the principal (seller) and must be stated in the listing agreement.

52. 1. A licensee may only insert required information into a contract prepared by an attorney. There is no mandated statewide contract in Maryland. Only REALTORS® may use the contract written by the Maryland Association of REALTORS®.

53. 1. The agreement says "after 90 days" so the broker is not obligated to buy it until the 90-day expiration and the broker must indicate all terms so that the seller is not surprised.

54. 3. The broker must immediately provide the buyers a copy of the agreement. Completing a false, second purchase agreement for the purposes of obtaining a larger loan is prohibited under any circumstances, and all written offers must be presented to the seller immediately.

55. 4. Maryland does not have multiple broker nonbinding listings. For a listing to be enforceable, it must be in writing.

56. 2. The maximum security deposit that a landlord can collect is up to two months' rent or $50, whichever is more.

57. 1. The age of legal competence in Maryland is 18.

58. 3. Sexual preference is not a protected class under the Maryland Fair Housing Law.

59. 4. After the contract is fully formed, earnest money held in trust for someone must be deposited promptly, which is generally considered to be seven banking days.

60. 1. The purchaser is bound by the conditions and terms of the lease. Right of first refusal is only required in Baltimore City.

61. 4. The stove was replaced as a result of normal age and life expectancy expiration. The security deposit can be used for unpaid rent, losses due to breach or violation of the lease contract, and the cost of repairs beyond normal wear and tear.

62. 4. Maryland does not allow a cognovit clause. The lease generally contains information on lease termination, termination time requirements, and provisions for a late rent grace period.

63. 4. Maryland does not have a Chesapeake conservation surcharge.

64. 3. A hearing board must consist of at least three members: one professional commissioner, one consumer commissioner, and a third commissioner from either side. The entire commission is not required to make up a hearing board with the exception of a claim that had been dismissed but recalled for review within thirty days.

65. 1. The powers of the hearing board are the same as the real estate commission.

66. 1. The broker must respond in writing to the commission, giving an explanation as to the allegations and suggested remedial actions, if any, within 20 days.

67. 3. Any member of the commission may file an exception to the dismissal within 30 days,. The entire commission decides whether to refer for investigation or dismiss again.

68. 4. The decision is considered final but may be appealed to the appropriate court.

69. 2. Notice must be served on the broker or the broker of the affiliate at least 10 days prior to a hearing. The notice is served personally or by certified mail.

70. 1. The commission may hear and determine the case; guilt or innocence is not determined automatically if the licensee fails to appear.

71. 4. The decision of the hearing board shall be considered the final decision of the full commission and may not be appealed further to the commission. However, the case may be appealed to an appropriate court.

72. 1. An aggrieved party of a decision of the hearing board, which is considered the final decision of the commission, may appeal to the circuit court of Maryland.

73. 3. Failure to promptly account for any trust funds can result in suspension of a license prior to a hearing. All other answers are infractions that may result in disciplinary action by the commission and can include suspension or revocation of license and/or a fine of up to $2,000 per violation.

74.  1.  A decision of the hearing board is considered the decision of the full commission and is final. The decision may be appealed to the circuit court, and the court may stay suspension or revocation only if bond in any amount up to $50,000 is posted.

75.  4.  Notice of the license suspension is sent to the licensee, the broker of record, and all REALTOR®/Realtist organizations.

76.  3.  The real estate commission is responsible to maintain the guaranty fund at a level of at least $250,000.

77.  2.  The commission must maintain the guaranty fund at a minimum of $250,000.

78.  4.  The commission may assess licensees an amount to bring the fund up to its minimum level of $250,000.

79.  3.  Upon payment from the guaranty fund, the license of the licensee giving rise to the payment is automatically suspended. The guaranty fund must be reimbursed the claim amount with at least ten percent interest.

80.  2.  The commission may issue a proposed order that proposes a solution to the affected parties.

81.  2.  The proposed order is for small claims of $3,000 or less.

82.  4.  The spouse of the licensee or the unlicensed employee, if that employee is alleged to be responsible for the claim, or the personal representative of the spouse of the licensee or the personal representative of unlicensed employee if alleged to have given rise to the claim, may not make a claim against the guaranty fund.

83.  3.  The key word is "may." The real estate commission is not required to do anything but may summarily revoke a license for failure to account for any money held in trust.

84.  3.  The maximum ownership interest that an associate broker or salesperson may have in a real estate corporation or partnership is 50%.

85.  3.  The person filing shall (1) submit a copy of the filing to the commission and (2) send a copy by certified mail, return receipt requested, to the principal office of the person against whom the action is directed.

86.  2.  Any adult member of the family of the deceased broker may carry on the business of the deceased broker for up to six months if he or she surrenders the license and pocket card of the deceased broker and submits any other information required by the commission.

87.  4.  Any adult member of the family of the deceased broker may carry on the business of the deceased broker for up to six months for the purpose of closing and terminating the business.

88. 3. Subject to other provisions, any adult member of the family of the deceased broker may carry on the business of the deceased broker for up to six months for the purpose of closing and terminating the business.

89. 3. To qualify for the license of a deceased broker and continue the business, the person must be an immediate member of the broker's family, have been licensed for three years, and pass the broker's exam, even if done without taking the educational hours required for the broker's exam. However, the 135 additional hours of continuing education must be obtained within four years.

90. 1. The new broker must first pass the broker's exam and then obtain an additional 135 hours of approved curriculum within four years.

91. 2. The maximum amount that may be paid from the guaranty fund is $25,000 and can be paid only for actual damages. Punitive damages or lawyer or court fees may not be paid.

92. 2. This individual must maintain an office in Maryland only if Pennsylvania requires Maryland nonresident broker licensees to maintain an office in Pennsylvania. It is a, "if you make our guys have an office, then we'll make your guys have an office" situation.

93. 3. The fee is $5, not $10. The broker must submit an application for a branch office on the correct form supplied by the commission, the identity of the manager, and a $5 fee for the certificate.

94. 3. The manager and the broker of record both have the responsibility to provide reasonable and adequate supervision to the affiliates in each office.

95. 4. Each and every office must have a sign on the door or exterior of the premises that is clearly visible to the public and contains one of the following appropriate words: "real estate," REALTOR®," or "Realtist."

96. 4. The Annotated Code of Maryland provides that unless otherwise negotiated in the contract or provided by local law, the cost of any recordation tax or any state or local transfer tax shall be shared equally between the buyer and seller.

97. 3. The buyer does not have the right to select the seller's brokerage firm, but does have the right to select the title insurance company, settlement company, escrow company, mortgage lender or financial institution and title lawyer.

98. 2. Maryland real estate license law is administered by the Maryland Real Estate Commission. There is no Council of Housing Matters in Maryland and the association of REALTORS® is a trade organization. The Department of Housing and Urban Development is a federal agency.

99. 3. The governor appoints the members of the real estate commission, and the state senate gives its advice and consent. The secretary of labor, licensing, and regulation also gives consent.

100. 3. There are nine real estate commissioners in Maryland.

101. 2. The professional member must have been licensed ten years immediately prior to appointment and have lived in the area he or she represents for five years. The professional member may be licensed as a broker, associate broker, or salesperson.

102. 4. The governor, not the secretary, has the authority to remove commission members for cause. The term is four years and the terms are staggered. All terms begin on June 1.

103. 1. The replacement member may serve for the rest of the term and/until a qualified successor is appointed.

104. 4. The chairman of the real estate commission is elected from among the commission members annually.

105. 1. Two-thirds of the commission is not required to meet and transact business. A majority of the members serving on the commission is a quorum.

106. 4. The secretary of labor, licensing, and regulation appoints the executive director from three nominations submitted by the commission.

107. 4. The executive director may not be licensed in any state as a real estate broker, associate broker, or salesperson. The executive director should be full-time, possess a broad knowledge of real estate, and be reasonably well informed of the general agency and contracts laws concerning real estate.

108. 3. The chairman of the real estate commission and the executive director are surety bonded.

109. 4. The executive director is reimbursed for expenses under the standard state travel regulations, as provided in the state budget.

110. 4. The commission may hold hearings and may administer oaths and issue a subpoena for witness attendance. The commission has no injunctive powers or authority over a nonlicensee.

111. 1. Citing the Title and Section of the Code of Maryland is not a requirement for filing a complaint against a licensee, rather, a simple stating of the facts in writing is required. The complaint must be filed with the commission.

112. 3. The relative who provides referrals must be licensed to receive a referral fee. A lawyer who is not engaged regularly in the business of providing real estate brokerage services is exempt from the license law as is a builder in the initial sale of a home constructed by the builder. A real estate license is not required for a business broker who sells no real property.

113. 1. An applicant does not have to pay for a credit report. The applicant must be at least 18 years old, have successfully completed an approved basic real estate course, and have passed the examination given by the commission.

114. 3. The real estate commission has no jurisdiction over unlicensed individuals. A court could impose a fine of up to $5,000 and/or a jail sentence of up to a year.

115. 3. The commission cannot send anyone to jail but may suspend or revoke the license, and/or fine the licensee up to $5,000 per violation.

116. 3. Real estate salespersons' licenses expire in Maryland every two years from date of issuance.

117. 4. A salesperson must pay $45 and have 15 hours of continuing education in order to renew a license in Maryland.

118. 2. The licensee may reapply for reinstatement up to four years after expiration but must also meet the other renewal requirements such as renewal fees, broker affiliation, continuing education, and paying a $100 reinstatement fee.

119. 1. Renewal for a salesperson is 15 clock hours and $45. The question states that the licensee received his or her original license two years ago, therefore, the licensee could not be an associate broker or broker, which requires at least three years of licensure.

120. 3. A licensee who is not exclusively commercial and has been licensed for ten or more years must have 6 hours of continuing education—4.5 hours of legislative update and 1.5 hours of fair housing.

121. 4. A license may be inactive for up to four years as long as the appropriate renewal fee is paid. Clock hours are not required for renewal on inactive status.

122. 1. The licensee has been licensed less than ten years so he or she must complete 15 clock hours for each renewal period, or thirty hours in this case. Since the licensee had already renewed through two license renewal periods, the licensee needs to affiliate with the broker of his or her choice and pay a $10 transfer fee to go from inactive status to affiliation with a broker.

123. 3. To transfer a license, a licensee must obtain a release from his or her current broker, the signature of the new broker, surrender his or her pocket and wall license, pay $10, and submit the above to the commission. A licensee may not use forms of a broker with whom he or she is not affiliated.

124. 3. This person may obtain a Maryland license by affiliating with a Maryland broker of her choice who may or may not have an office in Maryland. She must also sign an irrevocable consent and complete all the other regular requirements for licensure.

125. 3. Only a licensee may explain any part of a contract.

126. 2. Work of a secretarial nature does not require licensing when done under the supervision of the broker. Personal assistants do not have to be licensed but then they can not show homes or negotiate or explain contracts.

127. 4. A licensee must apply for licensure within one year of passing the state licensing exam or be subject to re-examination.

128. 3. A licensee must be at least 18 years old, be of good reputation and character, complete the 135-hour REC-approved broker's course, have been licensed for three years, and pass the broker's exam. Upon completion, the licensee would be the broker and therefore would not be required to affiliate with another broker.

129. 1. The farmer must obtain a license because he has not owned the land for ten years or more and he wishes to sell more than six unimproved lots in a single calendar year.

130. 4. A hearing board is comprised of one professional member, one consumer member of the commission, and another member that may be either a professional or consumer member of the board.

131. 1. A license may be licensed by more than one broker if they both agree in writing.

132. 1. The broker earned the commission since the seller accepted the offer. The deposit must be returned to the buyer, and the broker cannot take his or her commission from it.

133. 4. Both parties must have a signed written agency agreement and consent to dual agency. The company broker must also appoint two intra-company agents—one to act on behalf of the buyer and one to act on behalf of the seller. Compensation or commission does not determine agency.

134. 2. While the original agent no longer has an agency relationship with the seller, any confidential information gained during the listing must remain confidential. Agents must always disclose information about the physical condition of the property.

135. 3. Presumed buyer agency begins when the licensee begins to assist the buyer or lessee in finding a property.

136. 3. The agent may not disclose confidential information about the seller, who is the one that the agent represents. The agent can provide information on properties for sale in the area and give out mortgage interest rates. If the buyer desires representation, then the agent would supply information regarding dual agency.

137. 3. The buyer does not wish representation, therefore the agent represents the seller and there is no dual agency. An agency disclosure form is required at the first practical moment.

138. 1. Maryland law requires licensees to put all agreements that they help negotiate in writing.

139. 2. The listing must state the brokerage fee, be in writing and signed by the broker and seller, and a true copy given to the seller. Maryland law requires a property condition disclosure or disclaimer form completed by the seller, unless the seller falls within one of the exempt statuses. An expert's report is not required on the listed property.

140. 3. Both parties or principals must give their informed consent for dual agency in writing. The broker also must provide two intra-company agents—one to represent the buyer and one to represent the seller.

141. 4. The first-time Maryland homebuyer closing cost reduction disclosure is used with a contract of purchase only by a first-time Maryland homebuyer. Every other brokerage agreement would have to be in writing, have an expiration date, and state the amount of the broker's compensation.

142. 1. The seller must give permission for subagency. Agency and subagency are procured from the seller, not the listing broker or co-op broker. Since the buyer does not wish representation, the buyer is a customer.

143. 4. Maryland law requires sellers of one to four residential units to give either a property disclosure or disclaimer statement whether or not an agent is involved.

144. 1. If the purchaser does not receive the property disclosure or disclaimer statement before entering a sales contract, the purchaser retains the right to rescind the contract within five days after receiving the form.

145. 2. The seller would say "no" since the seller has no knowledge at the present time.

146. 4. Maryland law requires the owner to furnish to the buyer either a property condition disclosure or disclaimer statement for the sale of four or fewer single-family units. Even if the sellers choose to disclaim rather than disclose, they are still required by law to voluntarily disclose to the other party all material facts about the condition of the property.

147. 2. The agent's relationship to the seller must be disclosed to the buyer at the first face-to-face appointment. This disclosure must be in writing.

148. 1. Title 17-322.1 of the Business, Occupations, and Professionals Article of the Annotated Code of Maryland states that it is not a material fact relating to property offered for sale or lease that a homicide, suicide, natural death, or felony occurred on the property.

149. 2. One of the three ways presumed buyer brokerage is terminated is when a buyer wants to write a contract.

150. 4. A salesperson is required to make known to the seller that he or she is a licensee. The licensee acting as principal is not required to resign, use a third party, or obtain permission from the Maryland Real Estate Commission.

151. 1. Licensees are required to make agency disclosure at the first scheduled face-to-face meeting.

152. 3. The licensee owes a duty of confidentiality to the tenant who hired the licensee. The disclosure was a violation of this fiduciary duty and the licensing laws. Representation is determined by who does the hiring, not by who pays the fee.

153. 1. The buyer does not know what the buyer's relationship or the seller's relationship is to the salesperson. Agency representation is not about the property, rather, it is about the duties and obligations to a client and a customer. In this instance, a salesperson is required to give an unrepresented prospective buyer an agency disclosure notice at the first face-to-face meeting with the buyer.

154. 3. The licensee must disclose the cracked foundation but may not disclose the suicide.

155. 4. An agent represents a buyer as a presumed buyer agent until one of the following takes place: (1) either the agent or the buyer declines buyer representation, (2) the buyer wants to make an offer on a house, or (3) the buyer wants to see a house listed with the agent's company.

156. 2. Maryland requires the use of the agency disclosure form in every residential real estate transaction. A lead-based paint disclosure is a federal requirement for the sale of any residential property built prior to the target year of 1978. The law does not specify disclosures regarding high tension power lines or airport locations.

157. 1. The seller must consent to subagency and the buyer is notified that the agent represents the seller. A firm working with a buyer (but not entered into a buyer agency agreement with that buyer) is allowed to show houses listed with another firm only if the seller (not the seller's brokerage firm) of the house gives consent to the subagency relationship.

158. 3. A licensee may only be paid by his or her broker.

159. 2. Owners must register homes built before 1950 only once and pay an annual fee of $10 per unit. Owners of properties built between 1950 and 1978 have different requirements.

160. 2. Licensees must qualify for and pass the state exam and affiliate with the broker of their choice before providing any brokerage services authorized by their broker.

161. 1. Representation, except for presumed buyer representation, is determined by a signed written agreement between the client and the agent/broker and not by payment of fee.

162. 3. Since buyer brokerage has been refused and the listing is another company's, the salesperson is a cooperating agent and represents the seller.

163. 4. One of the three ways presumed buyer brokerage is terminated is when a prospective buyer wants to consider a property listed with the licensee's company. Thus, the agent represents the seller.

164. 3. Confidentiality requires that information gained during any period of representation, whether it be seller, buyer, or presumed buyer representation, must be held in confidence even after the settlement.

165. 3. An unlicensed assistant may not prepare promotional materials by himself or herself. The assistant must have the approval of the licensee for whom he or she works. The unlicensed assistant may answer the phone, forward calls to a licensee, assemble documents for closing, compute commission, and other general work of a secretarial nature.

166. 4. The REALTOR® brokers may submit the dispute for arbitration to the respective board or association of REALTORS®.

167. 4. There is no usury on first mortgages in Maryland.

168. 4. The usury ceiling on second or successive mortgages secured by real estate is 24 percent.

169. 4. The person responsible for distribution of funds from a settlement at which a transfer of title has taken place must deliver a recorded release of mortgage to the sellers within 30 days.

170. 3. The seller holding a second mortgage must grant a one-time extension of six months.

171. 3. Owners and sellers must provide the closing agent with their forwarding address and Social Security number.

172. 4. A licensee should not conduct a title search because that could lead to charges of practicing law without a license. Licensees may keep schedules, provide data, educate principals, coordinate inspections, and deliver documents.

173. 4. A lender may not refuse to give a loan to any person, based solely on race, color, religion, national origin, sex, handicap, familial status, marital status, age, geographic area, or neighborhood.

174. 2. The couple will most likely hold the property as tenants in common. Separated tenants by the entirety is fictitious.

175. 3. A time-share developer must register with the Maryland Real Estate Commission.

176. 3. A time-share developer must make annual reports until the developer own less than 25 percent of the time-share project.

177. 1. At or before signing a contract of purchase, time-share developers are required to provide prospective purchasers a public offering statement.

178. 3. Generally speaking, the purchaser has the right to cancel until midnight of the tenth calendar day following, whichever occurs later, (1) the contract date, (2) the day on which the time-share purchaser received the last of all documents required as part of the public offering statement, or (3) the date on which the time-share unit meets all building requirements and is ready for occupancy.

179. 3. The right of cancellation may not be waived.

180. 1. Maryland is not a community property state.

181. 3. Tenancy by the entirety does not continue after the death of one of the owners. It is considered to be ownership by one entity, an irreducible whole of one unit. If one of the owners dies, the surviving spouse would own in severalty.

182. 2. The owner/developer must register with the secretary of state before starting the process of conversion from apartments to condominium ownership.

183. 2. The age of majority in Maryland is 18.

184. 4. Maryland recognizes none of the legal life estates, i.e., curtesy, dower, or homestead.

185. 2. Maryland employs metes and bounds and lot and block, or recorded plat system, to describe property. It does not use the government/rectangular survey system.

186. 4. Cities, counties, special taxing agencies, e.g., MNPPC (Maryland National Park and Planning Commission), and the state all have taxing authority.

187. 3. After the completion of work, contractors or suppliers have six months in which to record a notice of their lien. From the date of the lien recordation they have one year to petition the courts to enforce the lien, if the petition was not included when the lien was recorded.

188. 4. Maryland allows one year for the mechanic or vendor to petition the court to enforce the lien.

189. 3. The .5% state transfer tax is usually split between the buyer and the seller; but Maryland statute provides that for the first-time buyer in the state of Maryland the .25% transfer tax will be waived and the seller must pay the remaining .25% ($180,000 x .5% divided by 2 = $450).

190. 4. Maryland requires 20 years of adverse use or possession for a prescriptive easement or adverse possession.

191. 4. Continuous use, hostile to the owner, must be established for at least 20 years to acquire title by adverse possession.

192. 4. Adverse possession requires occupation and possession of the property without the permission of the owner for at least 20 years.

193. 3. The sheriff may place the belongings on the street under summary process in order to evict the tenant.

194. 4. The landlord must place the money in an interest bearing account and must return the security deposit within 45 days. The landlord must detail, in writing, any deductions from the deposit. The tenant does not have to ask for the money; termination of the lease triggers the return of the security deposit.

195. 1. The lease for more than seven years must be in writing, acknowledged, and recorded.

196. 2. The homeowner has the equitable right of redemption; i.e., may redeem the property before title passes to the foreclosing creditor. The statutory right of redemption applies after the property is sold and does not exist in Maryland law.

197. 2. If the delinquent owner does not redeem the property within six months after the tax sale, the purchaser of the tax sale property may apply to the court for a deed.

198. 1. The .5% (.005) transfer tax levied by the state is based on the selling price of the property.

199. 3. A disabled veteran would have to pay tax on his or her house. Cemeteries, government buildings, and most schools are exempt.

200. 4. $250,000 x .5% = $1,250.

201. 1. Tenancy by the entireties extinguishes upon the divorce and converts to tenancy in common.